Gospel Gone Blues

Jimmie Ware

A Publication of The Poetry Box®

©2019 Jimmie Ware
All rights reserved.

Editing & Book Design by Shawn Aveningo Sanders
Cover Photograph by Miti via Unsplash
Cover Design by Shawn Aveningo Sanders

No part of this book may be reproduced in any manner whatsoever without permission from the author, except in the case of brief quotations embodied in critical essays, reviews and articles.

ISBN: 978-1-948461-21-4
Printed in the United States of America.

Published by The Poetry Box®, 2019
Beaverton, Oregon
ThePoetryBox.com

*To my beautiful daughter Nicole Ware,
my very heartbeat.*

Contents

The Gospel Truth of Jazz	7
Tragically Beautiful	8
Perfecting Chaos	9
The Ultimate Ascension	10
Men Cry Too	11
Scottish Soul	12
It's Over	13
Next	14
Broken Guitar	15
Brown Sugar	16
Bliss	17
Black Stockings	18
Baptized by the Beat	19
Some Like it Black	20
Facebook	21
The Website, 1998	23
Morning	24
Music	25
Heaven	26
My Liberian Connections	27
Women	28
Sheet Music	29
Nina	30
Uptown	31
Time	32
The Peaceful Beatle	33
Reflections	34
Simply Beautiful	35

That Marley Magic	36
Sacred Symphony	37
A Love Note for John Coltrane	39
Acknowledgments	41
Praise for *Gospel Gone Blues*	43
About the Author	45
About The Poetry Box	47

The Gospel Truth of Jazz

My hallelujahs are genuine
Like cornbread from scratch
No recipe needed
When my soul needs to be fed
Jazz feeds it
Surely my spirit was in Harlem
When zoot suits were all the rage
I sat in parlors with my shiny sophisticated French roll
Perhaps an enchanted gaze
Reciting words penned by Langston
Coltrane serenaded my mental
'Round midnight as we gather at his soul-soothing alter
Zora always strolls in late looking lovely lips painted for poetry
In this place hatred does not exist
We are above this as we worship the musical truth
Racism is for another day, not in this place
The Renaissance lives on like a classic song
Sax trumpets and unity filled the air
Feet will tap and facial expressions will be legible
Speak easy, love deeply, smile sweetly
Yes, we are bound by melodic beats
In this place we live life on the ones and twos
Tip your waitress, escape your blues

Tragically Beautiful

She dreams in vivid hues
Only to awaken to shades of gray
Hopes shattered to pieces
Words refuse to come forth
Tears flow endlessly as she smiles
She must gather her selves from the floor
Return to a nonexistent reality
She is tragically beautiful
Singing out of key
Lost in melancholy madness
Where is the blueprint for sanity?
Her soul aches for understanding
Her spirit screams for comfort
Her cypher is unbalanced
Who will save this modern-day damsel in distress?
The Fairy tale wasn't supposed to end this way
It was just her imagination
No knights no dragons
No fairies in a magical forest
No Prince to save her with a kiss
She lives in a very different world

Perfecting Chaos

She left the jalopy running loudly
Sputtering oil and dark smoke
As she ran back into the mausoleum of a house
Hurriedly seeking her silver cigarette case
Her laughter pierces the night sky
Tonight she will waltz with her demons
Serenaded by cryptic ballads in her head
Joyful confusion, temporary conviction
Gentlemen callers awaiting her wrinkled hand
They will whisk her across the floor
She will remember to be coy in a Bette Davis
Kind of way, she peers into a mirror gazing
At a strange reflection and she screams
Silently, for it is her soul in denial
No longer the belle of the ball
Daddy's picture shouts from the wall
Mother ghostly presence screams,
"Who's the prettiest of them all?"
Contrary to the fairy tales told
Pretty girls do grow old
Still there will be one last Mardi Gras
One last night of debauchery before the velvet curtain falls
She makes it back to the car
Carefully places a smoke between her red lips
She disappears into the February moonlight
After all the jalopy still runs

The Ultimate Ascension

It is the least of imaginings most deserving of our attention
The storms beneath skin no one is mentioning
Place your hurt upon this page
Begin the dissipation of rage
Romance is an overrated inflated lie
Love is not guaranteed yet we must try
It is not a novel with lovers kissing tenderly
Sailing on a river with a perfect honeybee in sight
Designer clouds whispering everything's alright
Love is being there when times are tough
It is going the distance when life is rough
Not walking away when the option is there
Much more serious than fingers in your hair
Love overcomes fears, tears and the golden years
Love remains when lust is gone
When the quintessential honeymoon is over
Love, more realistic than that elusive four-leafed clover
The ultimate ascension deserving of our attention

Men Cry Too

6'3 pillar of strength
His heart beats to a sacred rhythm
Strong rugged and handsome
Admired
Still situations yank at his heartstrings
Unable to speak his emotions
He retreats to a lonely space
Crystal droplets roll down his face
No one wipes his tears
He is very human indeed
We paint him hero inside a portrait
Where pain in not allowed
Let him breathe
Let him cry
Let him cleanse and rebuild himself
The weight of multiple worlds on his shoulders
Is a heavy load
He knows the stereotypes are false
Just as the hurt is real
He is not Zeus, nor Superman
Let him cry whenever the burden it just
Too heavy

Scottish Soul
—ode to Rod Stewart

I fell in love with his mandolin
A foreign voice so soulful within
I imagined myself sailing
Across the Atlantic
To meet my friend
As sure as the Chicago wind
I knew I'd always love his songs
He sang of handbags and glad rags
I shopped at thrift stores
He sang of planes and travels
To distant shores
He was blue-eyed soul
Eclectic and untamed
He is Scotland meets Motown
He spoke of downtown trains
The stories were so relevant to me at 16
Musical coming of age soliloquies
Falling in love to
"Tonight's the Night" on the radio
WLS-AM in the windiest city of them all
Still his music moves this old heart of mine
Knowing, he gave me a reason to believe

It's Over

Birds chatter outside her window
Like a sweet morning song
Sun rays beam through white lace curtains
The smell of coffee fills her senses
Slowly she rises from her warm bed
Slides her feet into soft slippers
She glides to the bathroom
Washes her face and turns on some jazz

Vintage Charlie Parker fills the air and she
Snaps her fingers and smiles
Next up Coltrane, then Nina Simone
Naturally Dizzy follows, then Sara Vaughn
What a line up!

She jumps in the shower still enjoying
The soundtrack of her life
She is feeling numerous neon hues
Her gospel has gone blues
She is ready to end the emotional pain
She is prepared to give back his name
The union will be severed by noon
She will be free … she is me

Next

Michael is gone
Prince too has departed
Mick is over 70 can't you tell?
Extremely agile and performing quite well
Whitney is gone yet the legacy of her music is incredible
Practically unforgettable
Here today, gone tomorrow
Time is merely a lesson we borrow
Make the most of your moments here
Sooner or later we disappear
What will you leave behind?
Were you considerate, loving or kind?
Did you help someone along the way?
Did your presence make a better way?
It seems many have tried
They say no one gets out alive

Broken Guitar

Sheet music gone awry
Lost notes in a midnight sky
All alone with a saxophone
No conductor
No trombone
She weeps in the third chair
Life feels so unfair
Audience gave thunderous applause
Symphony gone, lost cause
She plays through the thunder
Smiles past the pain
Knowing the hurt will come again
No more clef notes
She strolls slowly to her car
No love in her heart
Like a broken guitar

Brown Sugar

I am this bohemian-like poet
I am a redhead with strategic freckles
God placed them just right because
He likes girls, I read that!
Black girls been making magic for decades
Have you heard Aretha's moan?
Diana Ross & The Supremes
Were our original "Dreams"

Long before Beyonce & Destiny's Children
I admired Chaka Khan's unique style
I love Prince and Rod Stewart
The Eagles and Earth Wind & Fire
After all the true birth of
"Rock and Roll be a Black Woman!"
Tara Betts said that and I remember it well!
Sister Rosetta Tharp and her wailing guitar
Finally inducted into the Rock and Roll
Hall of Fame!

Thanks Mick Jagger for your honesty
You understood why we taste so good
It's our flavorful "Brown Suga!"

Bliss

Snowflakes drift in crisp night air
I watch him sleep
Dreads down his back
Across my pillows
Moonlight illuminates his skin
I admire the view
Sleep will not overtake me
My body yet tingles from our last encounter
He deserves rest
I will freeze this moment in my memory
Knowing it will serve me well
His touch was magnificent
Skillfully navigating female terrain
We made our own brand of magic
I imagine others call it love

Black Stockings

Many surprises lie under fur coats
Cold climates tend to bring out the heat in lovers
A warm luxury SUV and a frozen lake
Make for a memorable arctic night

Bright full moon lights up the midnight sky
A half empty bottle of champagne and passionate kisses
Ignite flames of another flavor
Black stockings with back seam moved him in ways
I was unaware of, the fur coat had to go

Black stockings, black seams
Black fantasy, black dreams
Kissing requires expertise
It is intoxicating to say the least
Practically magical under moonlight
Slow hands, just right
He whispers the right words
Pure delight

Baptized by the Beat

Some days I need to be baptized by the beat
Lost in jasmine scented clouds of ecstasy
I want to dance on tribal sands
With a Nubian man
With gifted hands
I want to be lifted a bit higher
Than my everyday norm
I want to feel cozy cared for and warm
I want to sing while making magic on a grand piano
Under a crystal chandelier until my inhibitions disappear
I long to feed him grapes
Correct mistakes, so we can mate
I want to love deeply, behave sweetly
As Maxwell plays repeatedly
I, adorned in cultural splendor
He will certainly surrender and sax slowly
Organically know me
Finding freedom in my eyes
We will become intense
His dollars will make sense
He will love me like a favorite song
His heartbeat, strong
I am no broken guitar
nor a cymbal to merely clang together
I am she the founder of Black Feather
Female go-getter, therefore, he must add to the equation
Making me even better, he must pray to a higher power
Shower me with love and affection
Grown women desire more than an erection
With no sense of direction, we require a deeper connection
The authentic kind, I need you to make love to my mind

Some Like it Black

French Quarter jazz
Soca in Senegal
Reggae in Kingston
I like it all
Esperanza Spalding's upright bass
Nina Simone in your face
John Coltrane smooth like brandy
As only he can be like Bob Marley
When Etta James sang At Last
Surely the spell was cast
Nancy Wilson, Sarah Vaughn
Minnie Ripperton was the one!
Aretha, Whitney, Patti too
Sonia Sanchez, Maya Angelou
BB King of all the blues
Azucar! The unforgettable Celia Cruz
Pieces of a Dream
Earth Wind and Fire
Rick James' Fire and Desire
Motown was where it's at
I like it like that and some
Like it black

Facebook

Why is she Facebooking the nation?
Private situations
Subject to strange speculation
Common sense on vacation
Senseless acts and tactics
Foolish acrobatics
Ridiculous and you want me to *like*
I cannot condone the hype
He checks in from everywhere he goes
Perhaps he feels the world should know
He's on the block, it's much too hot
Someone has a plot and it's too late to stop
They put their relationship all over the page
The good the bad, third time engaged
Is it real or is it staged? Click and look
It's all on face book
It should be a positive place
Pleasant cyberspace but it's become
A disgrace when arguments take place
He has a bad attitude
She is nearly nude
Someone's being sued
No one thinks first
Too much hunger and thirst
For public attention
Be careful what you mention
Heavy hitters deliver on twitter
Others chose to over expose
Anything goes, foul language, meaningless prose
Heaven only knows, the highs and lows

[. . .]

How much nerve it took
To publicize your inner-child
On Facebook

The Website, 1998

www. Inside
This web is girl-wide
Whenever he wants to ride
www. Him. Me
How's his hard drive?
I think I need to see
There is something he wants to install
First, he must stand tall and get through the fire wall
Because I want it all
The feeling is soft and wet on my intra-net
Feel the romantic sweat and continue
The main menu? Well, I thought you knew
I am pointing and clicking, sliding and slipping
For it is finger licking, good that is
Now he wants to send me email
With romantic details about me
Being a sexy female
With no time to waste and a mocha-like taste
I'm checking out his CD rom
Not just for high tech fun
I wanna www(dot)come
This program is all the rage
We are virtual panthers in a cage
So, before my baby exits
He will press save

Morning

Morning has broken and sunlight fills this room
There are trails of clothing and hints of perfume
I open the drapes, feed you grapes
Just to
Watch you
Open your mouth
The sight recreates my hunger
Makes me wonder
About turning you out or turning you on because its
Warm inside your arms
I didn't want to, but you're kissing my earlobe
And that's the spot
You may have what you've already got
This is a most elaborate plot
I will close my eyes if need be
Go ahead, I will count to three…

Music

Like the Supremes of yester-year
A symphony is what I hear
When he comes near
Playing melodies heard by the masses
Penned just for me
Let's not confuse this
It is simply divine music
As he plays for me key to key
My senses are soothed
My soul is grooved by this maestro
Swinging low to take me high
Like some lullaby not quite finished by Duke
Melancholy is my baby on this Sunday afternoon
As he plays a new tune for me to hear
It falls on my ear like a feather from the sky
The notes so sweet the get me high
Although I try to walk away
He strums me back again in the key of C
You and me, us, baby
His notes are mine, he gets my time
No matter how you choose it
For us it is no less than divine
Music

Heaven

He asked me to dance
Held me close
Heart beating overtime
His hand in mine
Slowly we moved
Across the floor
Imagining so much more
Gentle caress around my waist
A light kiss on my cheek
He adored the taste
Eyes closed
Everyone was gone
Just us two alone
Etta was singing something
I was delirious
He pulled me closer
I was curious
Six minutes of pleasure
I was captivated
It felt like heaven
Glad I waited

My Liberian Connections

Tropical waterfall
Palm trees and cassava leaves
Guinness flowing, music playing
Liberian girls simply slaying
Kind smiles
Fashionable styles
Sharp guys in fly ties
I like the way they dance
Cultural swag and romance
I like the way he moves
He's from the motherland
Blue skies and white sand
I love his
Hands

Women

Powerful than most believe
Everything we are
Everything you need
Wound healer
Hope dealer
Giver of life
We fly without wings
You steal our harmony
Still we sing
We cry when no one is there
We dance with flowers
In our hair
Renegotiate when life seems unfair
Creative and captivating
We make dreams come true
We are the light that shines
For you

Sheet Music

Sax me slowly
Pretend you know me
Whisper to me in French
I'll pretend it makes sense
Play me like a Spanish guitar
I'll let down my hair
You'll blow dreams into the air
Waltz me around the room
I'll be your bride
Not a moment too soon
Must we crescendo?
Tease my keys in black and white
You are my maestro tonight
I am your first soprano
Across a grand piano
A Steinway
Let's make love notes
Sheet music with candlelit silhouettes
Find our way to ecstasy let down your guard
Time to strike a major chord

Nina

Brilliant songstress
Activist on a piano with purpose
Misunderstood fighting injustice out loud
She screamed for us soulfully
Expressing our pain as racism ran rampant
Full lips spitting truth like a .45
Someone had to do it, her piano bled for us
She gave us anthems that will never die
Poetry will not neglect her legacy
She was in the midst of rights that were less than civil
Surely, she was familiar with injustice as a black woman
Natural beauty brown skinned warrior queen
I see her in black and white
The only hues in the real struggle
She was outstanding gifted and bigger than her afro
She was grace on fire!
Authentic vocals unapologetic messenger
She moved with the spirit of a thousand ancestors
Passionate about her people
Grace and fire, gifted!

Uptown

Six city blocks
Four hundred lives
83 cultures one high rise
Eyes filled with pain
No A game
On the B train
Ethiopian grocery stores
Selling Indian spices
Gang graffiti
Baked ziti
Laundromats and bars
Slumlords thrive
Crowded busses
The daily grind
Cities never even nap
Forget sleep
The beat goes on
Sonny and Cher were
Absolutely correct
Paradise was paved
Concrete is so unwelcoming
Flowers can't grow
The Sun Times
The hateful crimes
Luckily the sun shines
Thank God for the Lake
Vast and reassuring
If I ever get out of this place…

Time

She searches for a clock with no hands
Makes and conveniently neglects her plans
Turns moments into lifetimes
Turns wisdom into life lines
She slips away and you wonder where
The concept is neither here nor there
You were unaware
She moves swiftly beyond belief
She steals your hours not unlike a thief
She can be brief
She can give you comfort joy or sorrow
She cannot promise you tomorrow
She was certainly in your past
Now she's moving so fast
Just when you thought
She would last

The Peaceful Beatle

Sunday mornings meant
A hot family breakfast
And the Beatles
FM stations revisited
The evolution of the
Black suit invasion
Yeah, Yeah, Yeah!
John, was always my favorite
Even as he fell for Yoko
OH, NO!
Perhaps it was the round-framed glasses
Or his unique voice, just imagine
His lyrics spoke to my adolescent inner poet
Young emerging pubescent uptown girl
Striving to survive the vices of urban deterioration
One song at a time
Why must the peacemakers and undertakers
Meet so soon? John's lyrical genius soothed my soul
He voice embodied harmony
All he was saying, was "give peace a chance"
He seemed to be a catalyst for universal love
In a time where political upheaval was the order of the day
Thought provoking lyrics, unheard of and yet semi-comforting
Is there a prophet and musician in paradise?
Do they collaborate among the stars?
Are they playing heavenly guitars?
Marley and Lennon, imagine the concept up above
I dream vividly praying we all embrace
One love

Reflections

I see no reflection
Filled with uncertain direction
My heart needed protection
My youthful freedom, stolen
I thought I was golden
Like Phoebe's song, "At 17"
It wasn't all it seemed
Rarely chosen for the team
I picked flowers in the sun
Tried to be kind to everyone
I dried tears and eased fears
Always the dedicated volunteer
I gave back their names
They only caused me pain
I cannot find my smile
Misplaced my sense of style
What color are my eyes?
What happened to my hair?
Never been a flawless beauty
Sometimes life isn't fair
Fate you may not tempt me
My mirror is clearly empty
If only you could see much clearer
What happened *through* my mirror?

Simply Beautiful
—for Aretha

She was our rose, Cadillac driving
Queen surviving, soul singing
Notes ringing through the rafters
She was undisputed and stood her ground
Musician extraordinaire and profound
Never backed down in the face of adversity
Aries like me she was fire and took no crap

She put Atlantic records on the map
Understanding a woman's plight
Day and night better than anyone could
More than Dr. Feel Good
Today we are live streaming
I remember our queen day dreaming on wax
Soulful facts!

She was show stopping when mama was finger popping
She made us jump to it and rock steady baby
Miss Franklin was a dynamic lady, never a shrinking violet
Epitome of royalty, our beautiful Black Rose

She gave us all something we could feel
She was organically the real deal
She influenced generations from many nations

An American classic bar none, she will be missed
As she travels up that freeway of love up above
To that sacred place, golden wings upon her back
So long to Aretha's pink Cadillac
I look out on the morning rain
Music as we know it, will never be the same

That Marley Magic

His legacy lives through you and me
I forever adore his melody
How many little birds?
There were three
We remember his name
He did not die in vain
Wild dreads on stage
He engaged the masses
His lessons were not learned
Nor taught in classes
He removed our rose colored glasses
A natural mystic
On a mission
He made love a true religion
As sure as Kingston wind
His harmony lives again
He sang of buffalo soldiers
Dread locked Rasta
He was the real thing
Never an imposter
He opened his heart
He was loved by the world
The melodious memories live on
Like a continuous redemption song

Sacred Symphony
—for My Pops

Caramel fingers glided gently over white keys
I remember sweet haunting melodies
I sat quietly under magnolia trees
Bathed by a warm Savannah breeze
Summer sun kissing maple skin
I never mastered the violin
Lightening bugs dancing in the night sky
Never did I question why
Pound cake cooling on a windowsill
Cool winds howling at the pond
Grandmother in her garden
She and I had a special bond
Angels on earth don't stay long
Come Sunday I marveled at "his" choir
The only hero I could admire
Tall dark handsome and gifted
His finesse had us all lifted
His pre-rock and roll
Gospel filled the soul
Daddy played a familiar piano
Mama sang lovely soprano
His little girl, toothless smile, clapped along
Rocking back and forth to his gospel songs
Her daddy was larger than life
Beside him, a beautiful wife
Between them a red headed little girl
To her, he was the whole wide world
His keys yet play in my memory
Blues, jazz and hymns for me
He was everything a real man should be

[. . .]

My father was a sacred symphony
Like Marvin sang
"Mercy, mercy, me…"

A Love Note for John Coltrane

The second set was over and I showed no emotion as a
   seductive storm brewed beneath my skin in this smoky
   room of half empty glasses of beer
   His forehead drenched with sax sweat and his well-
   tailored suit wore him so well, he was jazz in human form
   and I longed for his sheet music

I sat quietly hair styled in a sophisticated French roll black
   seamed stockings adorned my crossed legs, red lipstick
   accentuating my sultry expressions for I dare not smile
   I absorbed every note knowing they were written for
   me I could feel the cadence of his saxophone sonnets
   translating poetically to my soul

He reappears from backstage and stands before a dark
   velvet curtain as the spotlight glistens on his handsome
   face he wipes his lips with a white handkerchief...it is time
   Lips to sax, heaven floats from his horn and I lift one brow,
   secretly tap one foot and politely refuse yet another drink
   from across the room

I cannot look away, his lovely notes command my attention
   with such musical finesse as he creates unforgettable
   memories for tonight time stands still and my heart
   applauds his genius, I sway softly as a subtle yet lovely
   tune fills this place, I am unable to prevent tears from
   falling as he deliberately invades my emotions

He is beyond beautiful, he is complex, spiritual and charming
   with a daunting presence, he is the epitome of musical
   devotion, how easily his *gospel goes blues* as I long to
   worship at the altar of his rhythm, after all that jazz

Acknowledgments

"A Love Note for John Coltrane" was first published in *The Poet's Haven*

Daddy, thank you for your music in my life. (Jimmy Pugh, Rest in Power)

Mom, you gave me strength and loving siblings. (Annie Hanna, Rest in Paradise)

Dr. Lorena Williams & Uncle Jimmy, All my love and Respect!

Gwendolyn Aretha Lewis and Rocky, you are everything.

Norene Ladd, my first fan and loving sister, I am proud of you!

Ray Hanna, I'm blessed to have you as my brother!

To my Nubian angels, Charles Reed, Laquanda Grant and Tamika White, you already know!

Cheers to all my Sister-Queens, Juliette Buford, Tara William, Neisha Jones, Zaneta Stetsunova

Andrea Antoine, Jaqueline-Lelani Hamilton, Rayne Di Martini, Wanda Henry, Arshella Williams

Dr. Ebony McClain, Dr. Rita Suiter and Rev. Marquita Pierre

To every Black Feather Poet, for gracing the stage or sharing a page, One Love!

Shelby Wilson, I could never have done it without your unwavering support and beautiful ink.

Mr. Walter Moy, A brilliant teacher who encouraged every student to succeed, I honor you.

Praise for Gospel Gone Blues

"Jimmie Ware's *Gospel Gone Blues* is a lyrical-poetic offering of and to those spaces between praise, pleasure and pain in which we all inhabit. These short, thoughtful poems are a wise woman's recognition that true wisdom comes with scars— and that the light that finds us after the darkest night is most beautiful when seen through the prism of tears. Ware's *Gospel Gone Blues* is an homage to the sensual aspects of loving and loss that only jazz can capture, and is itself, a musical tribute to those who have offered the poet their musical magic that has helped her, and many of us, transform our sorrows into symphonies and our howls into hymns!"

— Regie Gibson, literary performer poet, author, educator

"I fell in love the first time I heard her. Jimmie Ware has a magical way of weaving life into art and art into action. Her sweet words fall on your soul like the softest feathers, soothing any distress right out of your days."

— J. Ivy, award-winning poet, author, actor

"Jimmie Ware is enjoying the soundtrack of her life as she glimpses strikingly intimate moments and guides you from heartbreak to heroism. *Gospel Gone Blues* features Jimmie's relentless optimism and emotional honesty while escaping the blues, embracing the staccato of jazz and dancing through the tears with a playlist of passion, purpose, and personality that only Jimmie could bring to readers with such depth, honesty and energy."

— Stacy Eden, slam artist, poet

About the Author

Jimmie Ware is truly a *Poetic Soul*, which was the name of her award winning Anchorage and Chicago television show. She is founder of the Black Feather Poets, which honors her cultural backgrounds. Growing up in the Windy City was definitely a concrete jungle she survived. Jimmie ultimately became a freelance writer, community organizer, inspirational speaker, performance poet and advocate for suicide awareness with her Reasons2Live PSA campaign in Alaska. Her nonprofit organization was officially honored by Mayor Mark Begich, proclaiming February 27th as Black Feather Poet's Day in Anchorage.

Jimmie's poems and short stories have been published in numerous books including: *Chicken Soup for the Soul, Uptown Déjà vu, River Tales, Southwest Persona Poems, Vox Poetica* and *Open My Eyes, Open My Soul* which was the brainchild of Dr. Martin Luther King's daughter Yolanda King and Elodia Tate.

She has donated her time and talent to help victims of abuse, domestic violence, youth and women's empowerment. She is also an author for *The Good Men Project* online publication.

For Jimmie, poetry is like the air she breathes and a very necessary healing source for today's world and societal ills.

About The Poetry Box

The Poetry Box was founded by Shawn Aveningo Sanders & Robert Sanders, who wholeheartedly believe that every day spent with the people you love, doing what you love, is a moment in life worth cherishing. Their boutique press celebrates the talents of their fellow artisans and writers through professional book design and publishing of individual collections, as well as their flagship literary journal, *The Poeming Pigeon*.

Feel free to visit the online bookstore (thePoetryBox.com), where you'll find more titles including:

November Quilt by Penelope Scambly Schott

Shrinking Bones by Judy K. Mosher

Epicurean Ecstasy by Cynthia Gallaher

The Poet's Curse by Michael Estabrook

Surreal Expulsion by D.R. James

The Unknowable Mystery of Other People by Sally Zakariya

Impossible Ledges by Dianne Avey

Call My Name by Heather Wyatt

Bee Dance by Cathy Cain

and more . . .

www.ingramcontent.com/pod-product-compliance
Lightning Source LLC
LaVergne TN
LVHW020445080526
838202LV00055B/5338